D0712134

The Mating Game

The Mating Game

And How to Play It

Tips and Pointers
From the Collected Wisdom
Of H.L. Mencken
(Over Fifty Years a Bachelor!)
Edited by C. Merton Babcock
Illustrated by Charles Saxon

HALLMARK EDITIONS

Table of Contents

They are enormously dangerous and hence enormously fascinating.

The Hazards of the Game

It is the case with humans as with spiders: in both species the female is deadlier than the male. And a good thing, too. Every peak has been scaled and every ocean conquered. For men today, woman is the penultimate challenge. Each generation of boys grows up eager for exploring new frontiers. But Mencken would caution: "Fools rush in where wise men fear to tread."

The allurement that women hold out to men is precisely the allurement that Cape Hatteras holds out to sailors: they are enormously dangerous and hence enormously fascinating. To the average man, doomed to some banal drudgery all his life long, they offer the only grand hazard that he ever encounters. Take them away and his existence would be as flat and secure as that of a moo-cow. Even to the unusual man, the adventurous man, the imaginative and romantic man, they offer the adventure of adventures. Civilization tends to dilute and cheapen all other hazards. Even war has been largely reduced to caution and calculation; already, indeed, it employs almost as many press-agents, letter-openers and generals as soldiers. But the duel of sex continues to be fought in the Berserker manner. Whoso approaches women still faces the immemorial dangers. Civilization has not made them a bit more safe than they were in Solomon's time; they are still inordinately menacing, and hence inordinately provocative, and hence inordinately charming.

The most disgusting cad in the world is the man who, on grounds of decorum and morality, avoids the game of love. He is one who puts his own ease and security above the most laudable of philanthropies. Women have a hard time of it in this world. They are oppressed by man-made laws, man-made social customs, masculine egoism, the delusion of masculine superiority. Their one comfort is the assurance that, even though it may be impossible to prevail against man, it is always possible to enslave and torture a man. This feeling is fostered when one makes love to them. One need not be a great beau, a seductive catch, to do it effectively. Any man is better than none.

Suing for Peace

If a man pays $25 to a minister in order to get married, afterward paying $2500 to a divorce lawyer for the purpose of getting unmarried — how many times more precious is liberty than matrimony?

Hits and Misses

A gentleman is one who never strikes a woman without provocation.

When a woman is apologizing for her clothes, it is a sign that you haven't admired them enough.

Bachelors have consciences. Married men have wives.

No one ever heard a blonde say anything worth hearing; the most they ever achieve is a specious, baby-like prattling, an infantile artlessness.

Man weeps to think that he will die so soon; woman, that she was born so long ago.

A man's troubles usually wear petticoats. And even when they don't they should.

When women kiss it always reminds one of prize-fighters shaking hands.

After all women can keep secrets. Imagine them telling the truth about their husbands.

Women do not like timid men. Cats do not like prudent rats.

The whole order of human females is passing through a sort of intellectual adolescence.

Women Always
Want to Change the Rules

Watch out! Woman is an arbitrary and capricious sport who makes up the rules as she goes along. No sooner did she take up golf than she wished to move "her" tee fifty yards closer to the hole. The brand of basketball she plays is unrecognizable as the American invention of nearly ninety years ago. It is the same with the Mating Game. As Mencken observes, we might just as well say good-bye to the good old monogamous marriage.

It is women, not men, who are doing all the current gabbling about sex and proposing all the new-fangled modifications of the rules and regulations ordained by God, and they are hard at it, very largely, because being at it at all is a privilege that is still new to them. The whole order of human females, in other words, is passing through a sort of intellectual adolescence, and it is disturbed as greatly thereby as biological adolescents are disturbed by the spouting of the hormones. The attitude of men toward the sex question, it seems to me, has not changed greatly in my time. Barring a few earnest men whose mental processes, here as elsewhere, are essentially womanish, they still view it somewhat jocosely. Taking one with another, they believe that they know all about it

that is worth knowing, and so it does not challenge their curiosity, and they do not put in much
time discussing it. But among the women, if a
bachelor may presume to judge, interest in it is
intense. They want to know all that is known
about it; all that has been guessed and theorized
about it; they bristle with ideas of their own about
it. It is hard to find a reflective woman, in these
days, who is not harboring some new and startling
scheme for curing the evils of monogamous marriage; it is impossible to find any woman who has
not given ear to such schemes. Women, not men,
read the endless books upon the subject that now
rise mountain-high in all the bookstores, and
women, not men, discuss and rediscuss the no-
tions in them....

Sex is enormously more important to women
than to men, and so they ought to be free to discuss it as they please, and to hatch and propagate
whatever ideas about it occur to them. Moreover,
I can see nothing but nonsense in the doctrine
that their concern with such matters damages
their charm.... Charm in women, indeed, is a
variable star, and shows different colors at different times. When their chief mark was ignorance,
then the most ignorant was the most charming;
now that they begin to think deeply and indig-
nantly there is charm in their singular astuteness.
But I am not yet convinced that they have attained

to a genuine astuteness in the new field of sex. On the contrary, it seems to me that a fundamental error contaminates their whole dealing with the subject, and that is the error of assuming that sexual questions, whether social, physiological, or pathological, are of vast and even paramount importance to mankind — in brief, that sex is a first-rate matter.

I doubt it. I believe that in this department men show better judgment than women, if only because their information is older and their experience wider. Their tendency is to dismiss the whole thing lightly, to reduce sex to the lowly estate of an afterthought and a recreation, and under that tendency there is a sound instinct.

Game Points

He marries best who puts it off until it is too late.

When a woman says she won't, it is a good sign that she will. And when she says she will it is an even better sign.

A woman, once she is married herself, tries to snare a husband for her sister. A man, once he is snared, takes his brother behind the door and warns him.

Male Strategy

While Mencken was still a bachelor, he insisted that he believed in marriage and that he had "whooped it up for years as far and away the most sanitary and least harmful of all the impossible forms of the man-woman relationship." It seemed obvious to him, however, that the average male candidate for the honors of wedlock needs the best professional advice he can get before he takes the fatal step. Mencken offered such advice.

When a man plans to get married — and many a man plans to enter the matrimonial state, whether by instinct, hereditary impulses, tradition, or in the interests of what he believes is his future well-being and happiness, long before he has picked out the woman who is to be his wife — when, as I say, such a man plans to engage nuptial bliss he seldom if ever seriously considers what type of woman would be the best and safest, and not only the best and safest but the most beneficent, to take unto his bosom. Love, beauty, character, position — such things he meditates upon, but he gives no thought to subjects of much bulkier importance and, giving them no thought, often learns of them, much to his sorrow, when it is too late.

It is my belief, and I pass on the suggestion to

young men contemplating holy wedlock, that an orphan is perhaps of all women the one best fitted to be a desirable wife. The fact that she is an orphan automatically gets rid of the father-in-law and mother-in-law nuisance. She is alone in the world and grateful to the man who marries her. Having no one who is very close to her, her husband will seem closer to her than he would to a wife whose parents, or at least one of whose parents, were still living. Furthermore, the orphan is always the more tractable, wistful and tender woman. She has known sorrow, and sorrow, as the old saw wisely hath it, maketh a woman beautiful in the heart. But if the young man open to the lures and splendors of matrimony does not happen to love an orphan, but loves instead, shall we say, a widow, what advice then?

My advice then — and I may be forgiven for observing that it is grounded on a study of the problem ranging over a period of thirty-five years — my advice is to marry only a widow whose first husband either beat her or who died disgracefully, as by having been hung or by being shot in a bawdy house or by getting ptomaine poisoning from a free-lunch dill pickle. If the widow's first husband is *in absentia* for other reasons or by virtue of a dignified demise, she will begin to think of him and brag about him a few years after her second marriage, and that marriage will then quickly begin heading for the rocks. Only the widow who hates the memory of Spouse 1 can make a happy mate for candidate number two. But, yet again, if it is neither orphan nor widow that our ambitious young man has his passion set upon, what then?

Well, let us assume that the creature of our young friend's choice is a woman possessed of considerable wealth, and who is neither orphan nor widow. In this event my long years of investigation and research impel me to discharge the advice that our young friend consider marrying such a petitioner only if he himself be a very poor man. The marriage of a rich young woman and a very poor young man is revealed by the statistics to be generally a happy one, and for a simple reason, whereas the marriage of a rich young woman and a rich young man all too often turns out badly. The rich young man who marries a rich young woman gains nothing from the marriage, or at best little, in comparison with the poor young man.... There have been cases where a rich woman has kicked her poor husband out of the house, but so far as I know there has never been a case where a poor husband has kicked his rich wife out of the house.

I further always urge my protégés to marry pretty women. The best of women get homely all too soon, and it is well to have a pretty wife at least for a beginning. A pretty wife for five or six years is something: it makes, in memory and retrospect, romantic amends for the damaged wife one must live with in the many years that loom ahead of and beyond these first five or six years. The additional advantage of marrying a pretty girl as opposed to a homely one is obvious. The pretty girl will take out all her spoiled nature, whims and outside flirtations on her husband at the very outset, and thus get them over with. After a few years, when she loses her looks, she will settle down and behave herself, and give her husband no trouble. The homely girl, to the contrary, having no looks to fall back on or bother about, will begin by being twice as sweet and attentive to her husband as the pretty girl, but will end up by taking revenge on him for all the early outside flirtations that she never could enter into and enjoy and that, unlike in the instance of the pretty girl, thus never vouchsafed to her an opportunity to let off the steam of her vanity.

...I desire merely to add, in conclusion, that all the young men who have thus far followed my advice are happy husbands and fathers. Their wives never fail to remember me, with excellent cigars, at the Yuletide.

Men are not easily taken by frontal assault.

Why Blondes Have More Fun

Novelist Anita Loos admits that she wrote the first chapter of Gentlemen Prefer Blondes *in a fit of anger because she was in love with H.L. Mencken, who had just rejected her for a "silly blonde." That's the way the ball bounces in the Mating Game. Mencken gave points to brunettes for cunning, praise to redheads for perseverance, but gave his heart to blondes.*

If I were a woman I should want to be a blonde, with golden, silky hair, pink cheeks and sky-blue eyes. It would not bother me to think that this color scheme was a flaunting badge of stupidity; I would have a better arm in my arsenal than mere intelligence. I would get a husband by easy surrender while the brunettes attempted it vainly by frontal assault.

Men are not easily taken by frontal assault; it is only stratagem that can quickly knock them down. To be a blonde, pink, soft and delicate, is to be a stratagem. It is to be a ruse, a feint, an ambush. It is to fight under the Red Cross flag. A man sees nothing alert and designing in those pale, crystalline eyes; he sees only something helpless, childish, weak; something that calls to his compassion; something that appeals powerfully to his conceit in his own strength. And so he is taken before he knows that there is a war. He lifts his portcullis in Christian charity — and the enemy is in his citadel.

The brunette can make no such stealthy and sure attack. No matter how subtle her art, she can never hope to quite conceal her intent. Her eyes give her away. They flash and glitter. They have depths. They draw the male gaze into mysterious and sinister recesses. And so the male behind the gaze flies to arms. He may be taken in the end — indeed, he usually is — but he is not taken by surprise; he is not taken without a fight. A brunette has to battle for every inch of her advance. She is confronted by an endless succession of Dead Man's Hills, each equipped with telescopes, semaphores, alarm gongs, wireless. The male sees her clearly through her densest smoke-clouds....But the blonde captures him under a flag of truce. He regards her tenderly, kindly, almost pityingly, until the moment the gyves are upon his wrists.

It is all an optical matter, a question of color. The pastel shades deceive him; the louder hues send him to his artillery. God help, I say, the red-haired girl! She goes into action with warning pennants flying. The dullest, blindest man can see her a mile away; he can catch the alarming flash of her hair long before he can see the whites, or even the terrible red-browns, of her eyes. She has a long field to cross, heavily under defensive fire, before she can get into rifle range. Her quarry has a chance to throw up redoubts, to dig himself in, to call for reinforcements, to elude her by ignominious flight. She must win, if she is to win at all, by an unparalleled combination of craft and resolution. She must be swift, daring, merciless. Even the brunette of black and penetrating eye has great advantages over her. No wonder she never lets go, once her arms are around her antagonist's neck! No wonder she is, of all women, the hardest to shake off!

The Art of Camouflage

Women, when it comes to snaring men through the eye, bait a great many hooks that fail to fluster the fish. Nine-tenths of their primping and decorating of their persons not only doesn't please men; it actually repels men. I often pass two days running without encountering a single woman who is charmingly dressed. Nearly all of them run to painful color schemes, absurd designs and excessive over-ornamentation….It is color that kills the clothes of the average woman. She runs to bright spots that take the eye away from her face and hair. She ceases to be woman clothed and becomes a mere piece of clothing womaned….

How Not to Catch a Man

Mencken worked it out that if the average woman were as competent at getting a husband as the average car conductor is at robbing the fare box, then a bachelor past twenty-five would be so rare that yokels would pay ten cents to gape at him. He noted three major fallacies in a woman's logic respecting her attempts to snare a husband.

The axioms into which they have precipitated their wisdom are nearly all untrue. For example, the axiom that the way to capture a man is through his stomach — which is to say, by feeding him lavishly. Nothing could be more absurd. The average man, at least in England and America, has such rudimentary tastes in victualry that he doesn't know good food from bad. He will eat anything set before him by a cook that he likes. The true way to fetch him is with drinks. A single bottle of drinkable wine will fill more men with the passion of love than ten sides of beef or a ton of potatoes....If women really knew their business, they would have abandoned cooking centuries ago, and devoted themselves to brewing, distilling and bartending. It is a rare man who will walk five blocks for a first-rate meal. But it is equally a rare man who, even in the old days of freedom, would *not* walk five blocks for a first-rate cocktail....

*A single bottle of drinkable wine will fill more men with the passion
of love than ten sides of beef.*

Another unsound feminine axiom is the one to the effect that the way to capture a man is to be distant — to throw all the burden of the courtship upon him....A man face to face with a girl who seems reserved and unapproachable is not inspired thereby to drag her off in the manner of a caveman; on the contrary, he is inspired to thank God that here, at last, is a girl with whom it is possible to have friendly doings without getting into trouble — that here is one not likely to grow mushy and make a mess. The average man does not marry because some marble fair one challenges his enterprise. He marries because chance throws into his way a fair one who repels him less actively than most, and because his delight in what he thus calls her charm is reenforced by a growing suspicion that she has fallen in love with him. In brief, it is chivalry that undoes him. The girl who infallibly gets a husband — in fact, *any* husband that she wants — is the one who tracks him boldly, fastens him with sad eyes, and then, when his conscience has begun to torture him, throws her arms around his neck, bursts into maidenly tears on his shoulder, and tells him that she fears her forwardness will destroy his respect for her. It is only a colossus who can resist such strategy....

A third bogus axiom...that a man is repelled by palpable cosmetics — that the wise girl is the one who effectively conceals her sophistication of her complexion. What could be more untrue? The fact is that very few men are competent to distinguish between a layer of talc and the authentic epidermis, and that the few who have the gift are quite free from any notion that the latter is superior to the former. What a man seeks when he enters the society of women is something pleasing to the eye. That is all he asks. He does not waste any time upon a chemical or spectroscopic examination of the object observed; he simply determines whether it is beautiful or not beautiful. Has it so long escaped women that their husbands, when led astray, are usually led astray by women so vastly besmeared with cosmetics that they resemble barber-poles more than human beings?

Waterloo

The fundamental trouble with marriage is that it shakes a man's confidence in himself, and so greatly diminishes his general competence and effectiveness. His habit of mind becomes that of a commander who has lost a decisive and calamitous battle....

How Men "Pick a Winner"

Most turf bums know more about horses than men know about the women they're going to marry. A man who's going to put his life savings on a plug mare knows her height, weight, pedigree, track record, and how many good teeth she has. Few bridegrooms can say as much about the woman on whom they're staking a lifetime of happiness.

Men do not demand genuine beauty, even in the most modest doses; they are quite content with the mere appearance of beauty. That is to say, they show no talent whatever for differentiating between the artificial and the real. A film of face powder, skillfully applied, is as satisfying to them as an epidermis of damask. The hair of a dead Chinaman, artfully dressed and dyed, gives them as much delight as the authentic tresses of Venus. False bosoms intrigue them as effectively as the soundest of living fascia. A pretty frock fetches them quite as surely and securely as lovely legs, shoulders, hands or eyes.

In brief, they estimate women, and hence acquire their wives, by reckoning up purely superficial aspects, which is just as intelligent as estimating an egg by purely superficial aspects. They never go behind the returns; it never occurs to them to analyze the impressions they receive. The result is that many a man, deceived by such paltry sophistications, never really sees his wife — that is, as our Heavenly Father is supposed to see her, and as the embalmer will see her — until they have been married for years.

Is Woman Intelligent?

Sports are full of crucial questions. "Can Frazier last twelve rounds?" "Do the Celtics have enough height to beat New York?" Here Mencken answers an age-old question of the Mating Game.

That it should be necessary, at this late stage in the senility of the human race, to argue that women have a fine and fluent intelligence is surely an eloquent proof of the defective observation, incurable prejudice, and general imbecility of their lords and masters. Women, in fact, are not only intelligent; they have almost a monopoly of certain of the subtler and more utile forms of intelligence. The thing itself, indeed, might be reasonably described as a special feminine character; there is in it, in more than one of its manifestations, a femaleness as palpable as the femaleness of cruelty, masochism or rouge.

Psychological Warfare

She bets on the winning horse because it winked at her. He, on the other hand, has reasoned a sure thing, betting on a horse called "Seventh Heaven" in the seventh race only to see it finish between sixth and eighth. She can build a more incriminating case out of lipstick on his collar than the D.A. who catches a crook red-handed. How is it possible? Just call it "woman's intuition."

Men, as everyone knows, are disposed to question this superior intelligence of women; their egoism demands the denial, and they are seldom reflective enough to dispose of it by logical and evidential analysis.…But though every normal man thus cherishes the soothing unction that he is the intellectual superior of all women, and particularly of his wife, he constantly gives the lie to his pretension by consulting and deferring to what he calls her intuition.…

Intuition? Bosh! Women, in fact, are the supreme realists of the race. Apparently illogical, they are the possessors of a rare and subtle super-logic. Apparently whimsical, they hang to the truth with a tenacity which carries them through every phase of its incessant, jelly-like shifting of form. Apparently unobservant and easily deceived, they see with bright and horrible eyes.…

Grand Slams

Rule No. 1: Don't think because a woman smiles that she is necessarily pleased.

The greatest of all human arts is that of being indiscreet discreetly.

Once a woman passes a certain point in intelligence, she finds it almost impossible to get a husband: she simply cannot go on listening without snickering.

Adultery is the application of democracy to love.

The resistance a woman offers to being kissed may be proof of her virtue, but too often it is merely a proof of her experience.

Temptation is woman's weapon and man's excuse.

Marriage is based on the theory that when a man discovers a particular brand of beer exactly to his taste he should at once throw up his job and go to work in a brewery.

A man may be a fool and not know it — but not if he is married.

The female body is very defective in form. Compared to it the average milk jug is a thing of intelligent and gratifying design.

Women: A Scouting Report

Mencken's researches into the charms and attractions of a ravishing woman convinced him that a man succumbs to a pair of well-managed eyes, a graceful twist of the body, a synthetic complexion or a skillful display of legs without giving the slightest thought to the fact that a whole woman is there. The chief satisfaction a man gets from conquering a woman of noticeable pulchritude, he decided, is that of parading her before other men — like an expensive automobile or a door-knob factory.

The most effective lure that a woman can hold out to a man is the lure of what he fatuously conceives to be her beauty. This so-called beauty, of course, is almost always a pure illusion. The female body, even at its best, is very defective in form; it has harsh curves and very clumsily distributed masses; compared to it the average milk jug, or even cuspidor, is a thing of intelligent and gratifying design — in brief, an *objet d' art*. Below the neck by the bow and below the waist astern there are two masses that simply refuse to fit into a balanced composition. Viewed from the side, a woman presents an exaggerated S bisected by an imperfect straight line, and so she inevitably suggests a drunken dollar-mark.

Moreover, it is extremely rare to find a woman who shows even the modest sightliness that her sex is theoretically capable of; it is only the rare beauty who is even tolerable. The average woman, until art comes to her aid, is ungraceful, mis-shapen, badly calved and crudely articulated, even for a woman. If she has a good torso, she is almost sure to be bow-legged. If she has good legs, she is almost sure to have bad hair. If she has good hair, she is almost sure to have scrawny hands, or muddy eyes, or no chin. A woman who meets fair tests all round is so uncommon that she becomes a sort of marvel, and usually gains a livelihood by exhibiting herself as such, either on the stage, in the half-world, or as the private jewel of some wealthy connoisseur.

But this lack of genuine beauty in women lays on them no practical disadvantage in the primary business of their sex, for its effects are more than overborne by the emotional suggestibility, the herculean capacity for illusion, the almost total absence of critical sense in men.

The Libertine

A wife doesn't have anything to worry about, according to Mencken. While husbands may talk a good game and hint at playing fast and loose, most have neither the native ability nor the inclination for jumping into the arena of "contact sports."

The average man of our time and race is far more virtuous than his wife's imaginings make him out — far less schooled in sin, far less enterprising in amour. I do not say, of course, that he is pure in heart, for the chances are that he isn't; what I do say is that, in the overwhelming majority of cases, he is pure in act, even in the face of temptation. And why? For several main reasons, not to go into minor ones. One is that he lacks the courage. Another is that he lacks the money. Another is that he is fundamentally moral, and has a conscience. It takes more sinful initiative than he has to plunge into any affair save the most casual and sordid; it takes more ingenuity and intrepidity than he has to carry it off; it takes more money than he can conceal from his consort to finance it. A man may force his actual wife to share the direst poverty, but even the least vampirish woman of the third part demands to be courted in what, considering his station in life, is the grand manner, and the expenses of that grand manner scare off all save a small minority of specialists in deception. So long, indeed, as a wife knows her husband's income accurately, she has a sure means of holding him to his oaths.

Even more effective than the fiscal barrier is the barrier of poltroonery. The one character that distinguishes man from the other higher vertebrata is his excessive timorousness, his easy yielding to alarms, his incapacity for adventure without a crowd behind him. In his normal incarnation he is no more capable of initiating an extra-legal affair — at all events, above the mawkish harmlessness of a flirting match with a cigar girl in a cafe — than he is of scaling the battlements of Hell. He likes to think of himself doing it, just as he likes to think of himself leading a cavalry charge or climbing the Matterhorn. Often, indeed, his vanity leads him to imagine the thing done, and he admits by winks and blushes that he is a bad one. But at the bottom of all that tawdry pretense there is usually nothing more material than a scraping of shins under the table. Let any woman who is disquieted by reports of her husband's derelictions figure to herself how long it would have taken him to propose to her if left to his own enterprise, and then let her ask herself if so pusillanimous a creature could be imagined in the role of Don Giovanni.

He likes to think of himself doing it, just as he likes to think of himself leading a cavalry charge.

And the Game Goes On

Mark Twain, speaking of women's rights, once said, "I have never known a woman who wasn't right." Mencken would agree. He saw no reason why women should not liberate themselves from marital ties if it pleased their fancy. He doubted, however, that they can ever liberate themselves from their own feelings about men — that is, their interest in snaring them.

At the present time women waver between two schemes of life, the old and the new. On the one hand, their economic independence is still full of conditions, and on the other hand they are in revolt against certain basic and immemorial conventions. The result is a general unrest, with many symptoms of absurd and unintelligent revolt.

But romance — that is eternal. Whatever the future of monogamous marriage, there will never be any decay of that agreeable adventurousness which now lies at the bottom of all relations between men and women. Women may emancipate themselves; they may borrow the whole masculine bag of tricks and they may cure themselves of their great desire for the vegetable security of marriage, but they will never cease to be women, and so long as they are women they will remain provocative to men.

In the Trenches

A woman is as happy as she looks pretty. A man is as happy as he feels important.

Women love to believe themselves misunderstood. One never realizes this until one understands them.

Love is a game in which men play for the fun of it and women for the prize. Both usually lose.

Flattery is pretending to like the girl more than you like the kiss.

In every woman's life there is one real and consuming love. But very few women guess which one it is.

A woman always knows when a man is lying — save when he is telling a lie she wants to hear.

The great secret of happiness in love is to be glad that the other fellow married her.

The notion that women admire their men-folks is pure moonshine. The most they ever achieve in that direction is to pity them.

Many more men than women go insane.

Playing Dirty

Every contact sport has its casualties. The Mating Game is no different, though women seem to get the best of it. Probably, as Mencken observed, because they bite in the clinches.

Any man who is so unfortunate as to have a serious controversy with a woman, say in the department of finance, theology or amour, must inevitably carry away from it a sense of having passed through a dangerous and hair-raising experience. Women not only bite in the clinches, they bite even in open fighting; they have a dental reach, so to speak, of amazing length. No attack is so desperate that they will not undertake it, once they are aroused; no device is so unfair and horrifying that it stays them....

Many more men than women go insane, and many more married men than single men. The fact puzzles no one who has had the same opportunity that I had to find out what goes on, year in and year out, behind the doors of apparently happy homes. A woman, if she hates her husband (and many of them do), can make life so sour and obnoxious to him that even death upon the gallows seems sweet by comparison. This hatred, of course, is often, and perhaps almost invariably, quite justified. To be the wife of an ordinary man, indeed, is an experience that must be very hard to bear. The hollowness and vanity of the fellow, his petty meanness and stupidity, his puling sentimentality and credulity, his bombastic air of a cock on a dunghill, his anesthesia to all whispers and summonings of the spirit, above all, his loathsome clumsiness in amour — all these things must revolt any woman above the lowest....His performance as a gallant, as Honoré de Balzac long ago observed, unescapably suggests a gorilla's efforts to play the violin.

How to Be a Good Loser

It is indeed true that in any contest there is bound to be one winner and one loser. What of the outcome of the Mating Game? History offers a clue. Although it was Eve who ate the apple, the subsequent calamity is known everywhere as "the fall of man." Some guys just can't win.

And what is meant by falling in love? What is meant by it is a procedure whereby a man accounts for the fact of his marriage, after feminine initiative and generalship have made it inevitable, by enshrouding it in a purple maze of romance — in brief, by setting up the doctrine that an obviously self-possessed and mammalian woman, engaged deliberately in the most important adventure of her life, and with the keenest understanding of its utmost implications, is a naive, tender, moony and almost disembodied creature, enchanted and made perfect by emotions that have stolen upon her unawares, and which she could not acknowledge, even to herself, without blushing to death. By this preposterous doctrine, the defeat and enslavement of the man is made glorious, and even gifted with a touch of flattering naughtiness. The sheer horsepower of his wooing has assailed and overcome her maiden modesty; she trembles in his arms; he has been granted a free franchise to work his wicked will upon her.

...The truth is that, in a world almost divested of intelligible idealism, and hence dominated by a senseless worship of the practical, marriage offers the best career that the average woman can reasonably aspire to, and, in the case of very many women, the only one that actually offers a livelihood.

The Thinking Man's Guide to Marriage

What does one get out of marriage, anyway? After the ceremony, the reception, the honeymoon — the ritual paraphernalia...in short, after the dust settles, there is a general reckoning up.

A man in full possession of the modest faculties that nature commonly apportions to him is at least far enough above idiocy to realize that marriage is a bargain in which he seldom wants *all* that taking a wife offers and implies. He wants, at most, no more than certain parts. He may desire, let us say, a housekeeper to protect his goods and entertain his friends — but he may shrink from the thought of sharing his bathtub with anyone, and home cooking may be downright poisonous to him. He may yearn for a son to pray at his tomb — and yet suffer acutely at the mere approach of relatives-in-law. He may dream of a beautiful and complaisant mistress, less exigent and mercurial than any bachelor may hope to discover — and stand aghast at admitting her to his bank-book, his family-tree and his secret ambitions. He may want company and not intimacy, or intimacy and not company. He may want a cook and not a partner in his business, or a partner in his business and not a cook.

But in order to get the precise thing or things

that he wants, he has to take a lot of other things that he doesn't want — that no sane man, in truth, could imaginably want — and it is to the enterprise of forcing him into this almost Armenian bargain that the woman of his "choice" addresses herself. Once the game is fairly set, she searches out his weaknesses with the utmost delicacy and accuracy, and plays upon them with all her superior resources. He carries a handicap from the start. His sentimental and unintelligent belief in theories that she knows quite well are not true — *e.g.*, the theory that she shrinks from him, and is modestly appalled by the banal carnalities of marriage itself — gives her a weapon against him which she drives home with instinctive and compelling art. The moment she discerns this sentimentality bubbling within him — that is, the moment his oafish smirks and eye-rollings signify that he has achieved the intellectual disaster that is called falling in love — he is hers to do with as she listeth.

Uneasy Truce

No married woman ever trusts her husband absolutely, nor does she ever act as if she did trust him. Her utmost confidence is as wary as an American pickpocket's confidence that the policeman on the beat will stay bought.

Fire and Cross Fire

Women always excel men in that sort of wisdom which comes from experience. To be a woman is itself a terrible experience.

No man, examining his marriage intelligently, can fail to observe that it is compounded, at least in part, of slavery, and that he is the slave.

Any man is rich who makes fifty dollars more a year than his wife's sister's husband.

Jealousy is the theory that some other fellow has just as little taste.

Women have simple tastes. They can get pleasure out of the conversation of children in arms and men in love.

Whatever a woman genuinely wills, God discreetly agrees to.

Bachelors know more about women than married men. If they didn't they'd be married, too.

Men have a much better time of it than women. For one thing, they marry later. For another thing, they die earlier.

Afterword: This Man Mencken

Henry Louis Mencken was born in Baltimore, on September 12, 1880, and, in spite of a number of temptations to move to New York, he lived there all his life.

Graduated from the Baltimore Polytechnic Institute at the age of eighteen, Mencken landed a job as reporter on the *Baltimore Herald*. Finding his life's work at the very beginning of his career, he quickly rose by leaps and bounds to the position of a brilliant journalist who was not afraid to speak his mind. His bubbling prose and idol-smashing attitudes brought him squarely into the public eye, and he became a topic of nationwide conversation. Many Americans were offended by his uncompromising honesty, but, uncowed by their threats, he continued to expose sham and pretension wherever he found it. "I am against all tripe-sellers and false-faces," he said, "let the chips fall where they may."

With his vitriolic pen, the "Sage of Baltimore," as he was called, created a popular image of himself not unlike that of a dragon slayer with a meat cleaver in one hand and a sawed-off shotgun in the other. During the rowdy and rip-roaring 1920s, he won notoriety as a bogey man — a special agent of the powers of darkness — the very mention of whose name caused prohibitionists, tinhorn politicians, gospel fakirs, and other such "up-lifters," or wowsers, as he called them, to push the panic button. He had a way of upsetting the national equilibrium, and he realized that "the prevailing view of Americans is that I'd achieve a public boon by getting out."

In literary circles, the estimate was quite different. As leader of a rebellion which launched such writers as Sinclair Lewis, Theodore Dreiser and F. Scott Fitzgerald, Mencken was considered a veritable shooting star, a high-voltage power center, America's reigning intellectual. The *New York Times* described him as "the most influential single citizen" in the United States.

On August 27, 1930, Mencken married Sara Powell Haardt, a promising young novelist. The announcement was sensational news, since Mencken, for the first fifty years of his life, had consistently maintained that he would sooner jump off the Brooklyn Bridge than be married. "Why should I marry, who have no gift for it?" he once asked. "I elect to view marriage from a seat in the cosmic bleachers. I am a fan, not a performer. If I ever marry, it will be on a sudden impulse, as a man shoots himself. I'll regret it bitterly for about a month, and then settle down contentedly."

Mencken did not regret his incredible decision. He and his bride lived very happily in Baltimore's handsome Mt. Vernon Place for a scant five years before Sara died of tubercular meningitis. "It was a beautiful adventure while it lasted," HLM wrote to one of his friends. "Now I feel completely dashed and dismayed. No sensible work is possible."

Mencken's career was a colorful one. He himself was exuberant, boisterous, sometimes ribald, full of mischievous pranks, and capable of roars of laughter, mostly at other people's expense. As one writer puts it, "He was so delighted with the world that the daily miracle of a fresh egg for breakfast could stir his buoyant zest for life."

In the fall of 1948, Mencken suffered a cerebral thrombosis which left him paralyzed and incoherent for a time, but to everyone's surprise he woke up one morning and demanded, in his usual gruff manner, a boiled egg and a stein of beer. He realized, of course, that his days were numbered, and he said, "If I had my life to live over again, I don't think I'd change it in any particular of the slightest consequence."

On January 29, 1956, he died quietly in his bed. His work was done. He had blasted his way into the American consciousness as few others have been able to do. He had ushered in a new literature. He had carved his initials on one of the most exciting eras in American history. He had convinced a nation that it is perfectly safe to be honest, that nothing, after all, happens to the man who speaks his own mind.

Set in Goudy Old Style with display type
in Goudy Old Style Bold, a delicately styled
original alphabet drawn by the American
designer Frederic W. Goudy for the Monotype.
Printed on Hallmark Crown Royale Book paper.
Designed by Richard S. Peterson.